Where Animals Live

The World of Polar Bears

Words by Virginia Harrison

Adapted from Martin Banks' *The Polar Bear on the Ice*

Photographs by
Oxford Scientific Films

Gareth Stevens Publishing
Milwaukee

Contents

Where Polar Bears Live

The Polar Bear lives in the northern part of the world, where there is always snow and ice. This huge *mammal* is white like its surroundings above and around the Arctic Circle.

The Polar Bear has strong legs, heavy feet, a long neck, and thick fur. It is the largest *species* of bear — larger and heavier than any other meat-eating, four-legged animal.

The strongest *predator* of the Arctic, the Polar Bear walks long distances over its frozen home in search of its main *prey*, the seal.

When they have to, Polar Bears will swim many miles through the icy water of the Arctic Ocean that is part of their habitat. Although they spend most of their time on land, their bodies are adapted to this semi-*aquatic* life. They are *insulated* by a shaggy, water-repellent coat and a thick layer of fat.

Polar Bears often move with the drifting pack ice that floats in the ocean. The ice flows south during the winter, and north again during the summer. Sometimes the bears leave the ice for land, but they never go far from open water.

The *environment* in which Polar Bears live consists of subzero temperatures, short summers, and long winters. Few humans live in this remote part of the world, and until recently, all we knew about Polar Bears came from Inuit (Eskimo) people and Arctic explorers. Nowadays scientists can study Polar Bears firsthand.

The Polar Bear's Body

The white color of the Polar Bear's coat provides *camouflage* against the snow and ice, hiding the bear from its prey. Its coat is usually thicker and whiter in the winter than in the summer.

Adult male Polar Bears may grow to more than 9 feet (3 m) long and weigh over 1,400 lbs (650 kg). Healthy, well-fed Polar Bears may have a layer of fat under their skin as thick as 3 inches (7.5 cm) on their shoulders and hips. During the winter, when food is scarce, they rely on this fat for nutrition and protection from the cold.

The Polar Bear's Head

Compared to other bears, the Polar Bear's head is small for its body, but its neck is longer. It has an arched muzzle, small, fur-covered ears, and deep-set eyes.

The *carnivorous* Polar Bear has teeth designed for catching and holding its prey, and for cutting fat from seals. Polar Bears have a strong sense of smell, sharp hearing, and good eyesight.

Movement on Land

A Polar Bear can walk easily on ice and snow. Its wide paws act as snowshoes as it pads across the snow. On the ice the fur between its toes keeps the bear from slipping and sliding.

When it walks, the bear shuffles along with its front feet turned slightly inward, and its back feet swinging out to the side. Polar Bears can also run or gallop quickly over short distances.

Movement in Water

Polar Bears only enter Arctic waters to escape danger, to travel from one ice *floe* to another, or to reach seals on floes. Although they are strong swimmers, the bears cannot defend themselves or catch prey in the water, so they avoid swimming whenever they can. Who can blame them when the water is so cold?

Polar Bears "dog-paddle" with their front feet, and steer with their back feet.

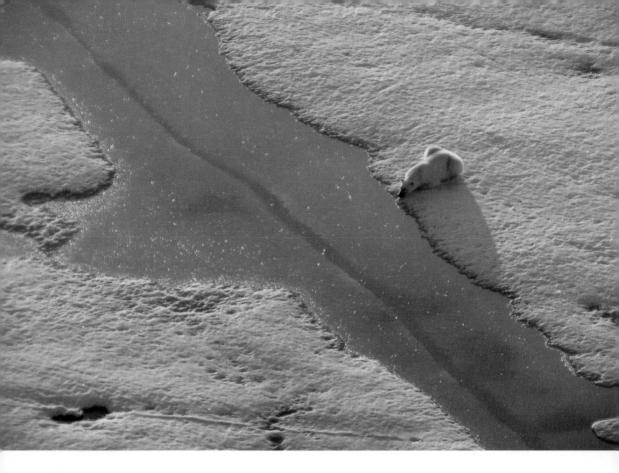

Food and Feeding

Polar Bears often catch seals by waiting until one emerges to breathe from an open "lead," or crack, in the ice (above). Unless the bear is extremely hungry, it eats only the seal's blubber and intestines. *Scavengers* eat the rest. Polar Bears may also eat dead Walrus or whales that have been washed ashore.

When the ice recedes northward during the brief summer, Polar Bears move onto land, where they switch to an *omnivorous* diet of plants, small mammals, birds, and bird eggs.

↑

When Ringed Seal pups are born in the spring, Polar Bears use their excellent sense of smell to detect them. The bears can smell seals through the icy roof of their dens, so they stomp hard on the ice with their feet and make the den cave in.

Polar Bears hunt adult seals that rest on top of the ice. In order to avoid being seen by its prey, a Polar Bear will flatten itself onto the ice and pull its body forward with its front paws.

Staying Warm and Keeping Cool

Polar Bears live in subzero Arctic temperatures, so they must be well adapted to protect themselves. A thick layer of fat insulates the bear, and hollow hairs channel the Sun's ultraviolet light through to the bear's black skin.

Many Polar Bears will go into *hibernation* during the coldest months. They each dig a den in snow near a sheltered area and sleep until the temperature rises. Those that do not hibernate can pull their legs under them, so there is less surface area exposed to the cold air.

↑

During the summer, the temperature of the Arctic land can reach 70°F (21°C), and the Polar Bears then need to cool off. They spread themselves out and expose more of their bodies to the air to let heat escape. They also dig out dens in the snow to shelter themselves from sunlight and insects.

Another way Polar Bears keep cool is through a network of tiny blood vessels in the muscle of their backs. During warm weather these vessels carry blood closer to the surface of the skin. This allows heat to escape into the atmosphere.

Courtship and Mating

At five or six years of age, Polar Bears are fully grown and ready to have young of their own.

When Polar Bears emerge from hibernation in the spring, they begin looking for a mate. When they are ready to mate, females produce a scent that acts as a signal to males. These young male Polar Bears "playfight" (below). But one day they may have to fight seriously with another male for the right to mate with a female.

In April or May, a male and female Polar Bear cautiously meet in courtship before mating. After mating, they may spend a brief time together, but the male's role in raising a family is over. He will leave, possibly mating with other females before returning to his solitary life.

After mating, it takes several months before the fertilized egg becomes attached to the *uterus* of the female Polar Bear and begins to develop. This kind of *pregnancy* is unusual, and it means the young are tiny and undeveloped at birth.

Birth of the Young

At the start of winter, the female Polar Bear looks for a sheltered area, like a large snowdrift, and digs a tunnel into the snow. At the end of the tunnel, she makes a cozy oval-shaped den. The wind soon blows snow across the entrance, and the den is hidden from view. The only opening is the small hole right above the female's head which is formed by her warm breath.

While the wind blows and the temperature dips to -50° to -60°F (-45° to -50°C), the den is quiet and warm. Here, after only a few weeks of pregnancy, the female Polar Bear gives birth to one, two, or sometimes three cubs.

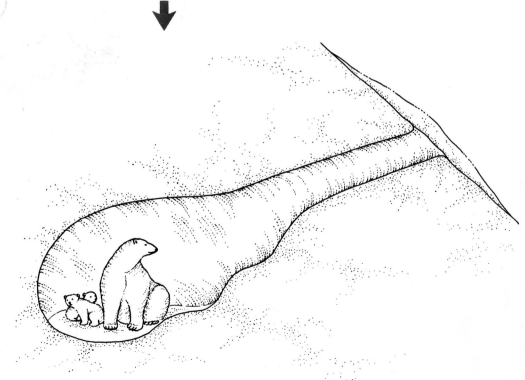

The new cubs are the size of guinea pigs and weigh only about 25 oz (700 g) each. They are blind and hairless for the first few weeks, and they spend their time nestled against their mother's fur, suckling her milk and sleeping. When they finally emerge from the den in the spring, they have grown much larger (above).

Caring for the Cubs

By early spring, the cubs are much larger. Their eyes are open and their bodies are covered with soft, white fur. They like to play and explore, and so the mother scratches snow from the walls to enlarge the den. Then one day, the mother decides it is time to break out of the den and into the open air.

Although the Polar Bear cubs like to play in the Arctic snow, their mother is still their only protection. They rely on her for shelter, milk, warmth, and safety. The mother tries to avoid meeting other bears, especially adult males, for they will sometimes kill young cubs.

The family stays close to the den for a week or more, and the mother often takes her cubs back inside. When she is fully alert and the cubs are ready, the mother begins the search for food.

Leaving the Den

After a week or two, the Polar Bear family is ready to leave the den for good. As the bears emerge from their snowy dens, their main prey, Ringed Seals, are also giving birth.

The mother bear sets out for the ice where she can hunt seals, and the cubs follow. They may have to travel long distances through the snow, and the mother stops often so her cubs can ➡ suckle milk and rest.

As they grow, the cubs learn to eat meat and to chew on the blubber of the seals the mother kills. Later the cubs watch as she catches seals at breathing holes in the ice, and, reluctantly, they learn how to swim in the icy Arctic seas.

Until they are at least two years old, Polar Bear cubs remain with their mother. During this time, the cubs travel with her and learn hunting skills in the summer and rest in the den with her in the winter. When they are almost fully grown, their mother leaves them to start a new Polar Bear family.

Migration and Travel

Polar Bears wander hundreds of miles each year. In the spring, when Polar Bears search for Ringed Seal dens, they may travel more than 25 miles (40 km) each day on the ice. Ocean currents and drifting ice have created huge walls of ice blocks called pressure ridges. The movements of the ice also create long channels of water called "leads." Here, bears find their seal prey. In the course of their hunting, Polar Bears may also drift on ice floes. This is one way of covering hundreds of miles!

While the bears travel and drift, they remain in certain areas of the Arctic and form small, separate *populations*. One population lives in Canada's Hudson Bay, which is farther south than any other Polar Bear home. When the ice melts in the bay, the bears are forced onto land.

Polar Bears *migrate* with the movement of the ice. The ice moves southward with the onset of winter, and so do most of the bears.

Polar Bears and People

Ever since people have traveled to the Arctic,
they have always met with the mighty Polar
Bear. The Inuit and other Arctic natives
depended on its skin and meat to survive in
the frozen North.

Although they can certainly be dangerous when
threatened, Polar Bears usually ignore people.
But early explorers to the North told of the
Polar Bear's ferocity and cunning. And sadly,
as more people came to the Arctic, many Polar
Bears were needlessly killed.

During the 1950s, Polar Bears were hunted from aircraft. Polar Bear hunting became so popular in Alaska and Canada that more than 1,000 bears were killed each year. In 1973, all the countries with Polar Bear populations signed an agreement to restrict Polar Bear hunting.

In the Canadian town of Churchill, Polar Bears scavenge for food at garbage dumps while waiting for Hudson Bay to freeze. Residents have learned to tolerate the bears' appearance every fall, and the town is now known for their visits. You can even study them up close from "bearproof" vehicles.

Polar Bears and Other Animals

Polar Bears share their Arctic home with a variety of animals. One, the Walrus, can weigh over a ton and measure 16 1/2 ft (5 m) long. Its long ivory *tusks* discourage the Polar Bear from attacking it. This large relative of the seal may even, at times, kill a bear.

The black and white Killer Whale may also attack a swimming Polar Bear.

On land, the Polar Bear is often followed by the Arctic Fox. The foxes scavenge the remains of a bear kill. In fact, they rely on these leftovers for most of their food, so they remain at a respectful distance from the Polar Bear until it has finished. Gulls and ravens are not so polite. These scavenger seabirds also join the feast — often before the Polar Bear has finished!

In addition to the *marine* mammals — seals, whales, and *even* dolphins — the rich water of the Arctic is home to fish and tiny plankton.

Life on the Ice

Although it avoids Walrus and Killer Whales, the Polar Bear is the *dominant* species of the Arctic and has few natural enemies — except humans. The bears hunt seals and other mammals, and scavenge dead whales and Walrus. These animals, in turn, eat smaller fish; the smaller fish eat plankton. On land, Polar Bears eat plants and animals. The "King of the Arctic" is at the top of the Arctic food chain.

Food Chain

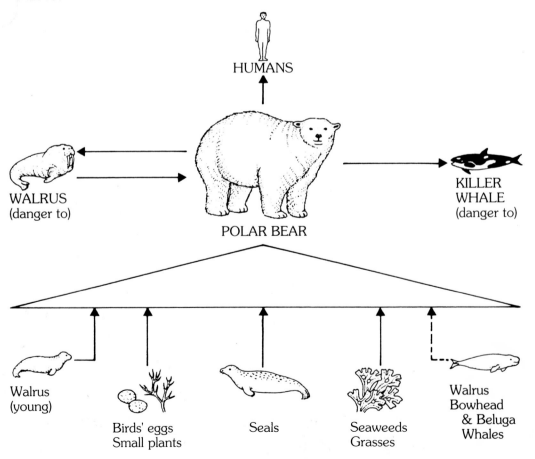

HUMANS

WALRUS
(danger to)

POLAR BEAR

KILLER
WHALE
(danger to)

Walrus
(young)

Birds' eggs
Small plants

Seals

Seaweeds
Grasses

Walrus
Bowhead
& Beluga
Whales

— — —Dead animals (carrion)

This unthreatened life may change, because human industry is moving northward. Our use of the Arctic's natural resources can seriously upset the balance of its *ecology*. The *pollution* that industry creates can disturb the richness of the Arctic Ocean, and in turn upset the entire food chain, right up to the Polar Bear. How we decide to treat this environment will determine how well Arctic wildlife — including roughly 20,000 Polar Bears — will continue to freely roam the ice and swim the seas.

Index and New Words About Polar Bears

These new words about Polar Bears appear in the text on the pages shown after each definition. Each new word first appears in the text in *italics*, just as it appears here.

Reading level analysis: FRY 4, FLESCH 85 (easy), RAYGOR 3.5, FOG 5, SMOG 3

Library of Congress Cataloging-in-Publication Data

Harrison, Virginia, 1966-
    The world of polar bears / words by Virginia Harrison ; adapted from Martin Banks' The polar bear on the ice ; photographs by Oxford Scientific Films.
        p. cm. — (Where animals live)
    Includes index.
    Summary: Describes in brief text and illustrations the lives of polar bears in their natural settings showing how they feed, defend themselves, and breed.
    ISBN 0-8368-0139-3
    1. Polar bear—Juvenile literature. [1. Polar bear. 2. Bears.] I. Banks, Martin, 1947- Polar bear on the ice. II. Oxford Scientific Films. III. Title. IV. Series.
QL737.C27H394   1989
599.74'446—dc20   89-4470

North American edition first published in 1989 by Gareth Stevens, Inc., 7317 West Green Tree Road, Milwaukee, WI 53223, USA. US edition, this format, copyright © 1989 by Gareth Stevens, Inc. Text copyright © 1989 by Gareth Stevens, Inc. **All rights reserved. No part of this book may be reproduced in any form or by any means without permission in writing from Gareth Stevens, Inc.** First conceived, designed, and produced by Belitha Press Ltd., London, as **The Polar Bear on the Ice**, with an original text copyright by Oxford Scientific Films. Format copyright by Belitha Press Ltd.

Series Editor: Mark J. Sachner. Art Director: Treld Bicknell. Design: Naomi Games. Line Drawings: Lorna Turpin.

The authors and publishers wish to thank the following for permission to reproduce copyright material: **Oxford Scientific Films Ltd.** for front cover, pp. 2, 6, 7 both, 8, 14, 15, 16, 17, 25, 31 (**Tom Ulrich**); title page, pp. 3, 21, 24, 27, back cover (Maurice R. Carlisle); pp. 4, 10 (Animals Animals — E. R. Degginger); pp. 9, 13 both (Mike Salisbury); pp. 11, 19 (Animals Animals — Margot Conte); p. 12 (Hugh Miles); p. 26 (Animals Animals — John Nees); p. 28 above (Animals Animals — Johnny Johnson); p. 28 below (Doug Allan); p. 29 (Carsten R. Oleson); Bruce Coleman Limited for pp. 20 (Thor Larsen), 22, and 23 (B. & C. Alexander).

Printed in the United States of America
1 2 3 4 5 6 7 8 9 95 94 93 92 91 90 89

For a free color catalog describing Gareth Stevens' list of high-quality children's books call 1 (800) 433-0942